The Picture Life of
BOBBY ORR

THE PICTURE LIFE OF

Bobby Orr

BY AUDREY EDWARDS
AND GARY WOHL

FRANKLIN WATTS | NEW YORK | LONDON | 1976

The authors are grateful to the publisher for permission to quote from **Bobby Orr: My Game** by Bobby Orr with Mark Mulvoy. Copyright © 1974 by Bobby Orr Enterprises, Limited. Published by Little, Brown and Company.

Library of Congress Cataloging in Publication Data

Edwards, Audrey.
    The picture life of Bobby Orr.

    SUMMARY: Brief text and photographs present the life of Bobby Orr, star of the Boston Bruins hockey team.
    1. Orr, Bobby, 1948–   — Juvenile literature.
2. Hockey — Juvenile literature. [1. Orr, Bobby, 1948–   2. Hockey — Biography] I. Wohl, Gary, joint author. II. Title.
GV848.5.07E38   796.9'62'0924 [B] [92]   76–16200
ISBN 0–531–01208–5

Photographs courtesy of:
Ken Regan, Camera 5: p. vi; Al Ruelle (Team Photographer, Boston Bruins): pp. 2, 3, 4, 7, 8, 14, 17, 18, 21, 22, 24, 25, 27, 28, 31, 35, 36, 38, 39; Pictorial Parade: pp. 10, 13; United Press International: pp. 32, 40.

Cover photo and frontispiece by Neil Leifer for **Sports Illustrated** © Time Inc.

The Picture Life of
BOBBY ORR

Every once in a while a great athlete comes along. This is someone who can do everything in a game well. Bobby Orr is such an athlete. He has been playing hockey almost all of his life. Many people think he is the best player ever.

Bobby Orr may be the greatest player in the history of hockey. Here he gets ready to make a pass.

There is an unusual thing about Bobby. He can play both the defense and forward positions very well.

Bobby in a good defense move.

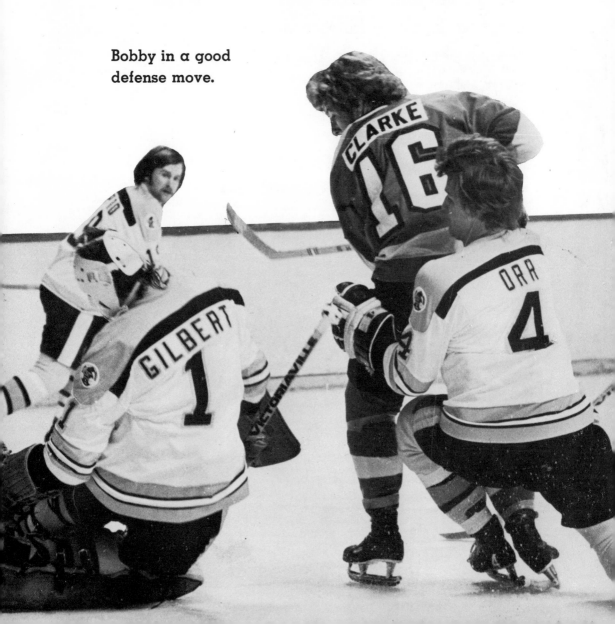

As a defense player, he has to keep the other team from getting the puck into his team's net. But he can also score as well as the forwards do.

Here Bobby rams the puck into the net to score.

There is a secret to being a good player, Bobby says. It is being able to skate well. "If you cannot skate, you cannot play hockey," he says. "It's the single most important part of the game."

Bobby was only four when he got his first pair of skates. They were given to him by a friend of his father's. They didn't cost very much, and they were too big. "They were my skates," says Bobby, "and boy, was I ever happy!"

Being fast on his skates helps Bobby to keep the puck in front of him while stickhandling.

Bobby joined the Boston Bruins hockey team in 1966. He was only 18 and had not finished high school. The managers of the Boston Bruins wanted to get him on the team so much, they could hardly wait for him to be 18!

Bobby at 18, on his way to becoming a superstar. Everybody in the stands seems to be keeping an eye on him.

Bobby has been playing hockey ever since he was a little boy. He and his friends used to play together in Parry Sound. This is a small town in Ontario, Canada. Bobby was born there on March 20, 1948.

Doug Orr, Bobby's father, had been a hockey player, too. He knew his son had the makings of a great player. When Bobby was only 10, his father took him to play in hockey games against grown men in the town. These men were sometimes as much as 25 years old. But they had trouble getting the puck away from Bobby.

Bobby's father is very proud. He remembers when his son practiced shooting every day in the family's garage.

By the time he was 11, Bobby was playing with the 14-year-old boys on the Parry Sound Bantams team. In 1960 the Bantams team went to play in the Ontario championship games. Some men from the Boston Bruins were also there. They were looking for good young players who might be ready to play for the Bruins in a few years.

Bobby, when he was 16 years old.

Bobby caught the men's eyes right away during the first game. He kept stealing the puck from the other team. He skated in circles to throw the other team off. He snapped shots at the net.

The men from Boston were really surprised. Who was this boy? Had any other big team signed him up?

The men talked Bobby's parents into letting him come to play for the Bruins' junior team — the Oshawa Generals. The junior team is often called the minor team. It is where many young players often start. When they are old enough, the best ones are chosen to play for the big team, called the major team.

The men from the Boston Bruins wanted Bobby to play for the Oshawa Generals as soon as he was 14. But they had to do a lot of talking to get Bobby's parents to let him play.

Bobby comes from a close family. His parents didn't want to see him going so far away from home to play on the minor team.

But Bobby's family also knew that the game was Bobby's greatest love. Finally, his parents agreed to let him play for the Oshawa Generals. The men from the Bruins were glad. This meant that Bobby could now play for the Bruins when he was 18.

Bobby (on the right) was the youngest player on the team.

When Bobby became 18, he was a better player than many players who were on major teams. Coaches everywhere knew it. He played good defense. And he could play forward. He was also fast. Other teams would have been glad to have him play for them. This meant he could get better pay from the Bruins if he agreed to play for them.

At 170 pounds and 5'11"
Bobby was thought to be
small for a defenseman.

Before Bobby joined the Bruins, the National Hockey League did not pay players very well. Their pay was less than the pay of players in other sports.

Bobby changed all that. He said he would play for the Bruins. But he had a good lawyer with him to make sure he would get good pay. Bobby signed a two-year contract. It also had an extra payment. In all, he got about $70,000. This was a lot for a hockey player! With Bobby leading the way, other hockey players could now ask for more money to play.

Bobby signing a contract for another season with the Boston Bruins.

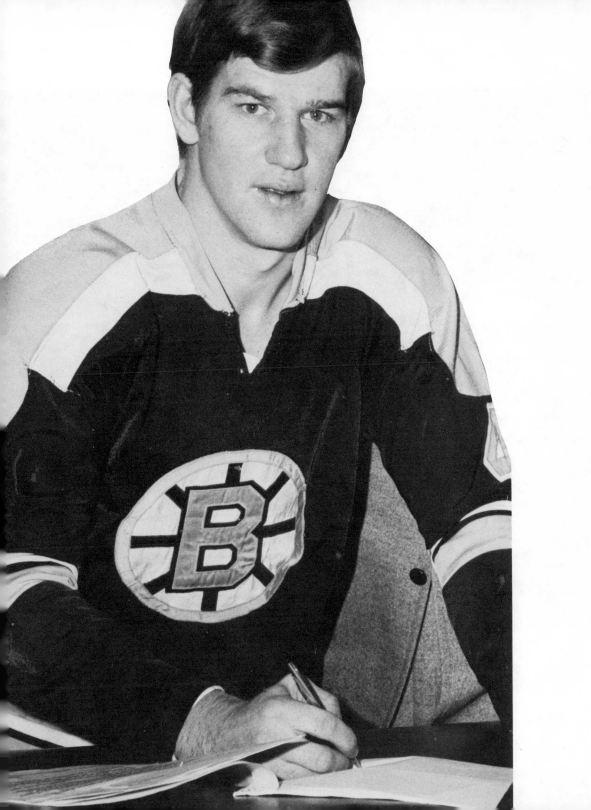

When Bobby signed to play with the
Bruins, the team was in the next-to-last
place in the league. This meant it
had won less games than other teams.
Fans in Boston called Bobby the "boy
wonder." They thought he would pull
the team up. He didn't disappoint the
fans.

Bobby is in this picture of
the Boston Bruins team.
Look in the second row.

His first game was during the 1966-67 season, against the Detroit Red Wings. Bobby kept the Red Wings from scoring by taking the puck away from them during the game. Boston won the game 6 to 2. Bobby helped make one goal by a good pass to another Boston player. The fans went wild and cheered him for many minutes.

Bobby keeps a player on the Detroit Red Wings team from scoring. Goalie Gerry Cheevers drops to the ice and covers the puck. This is in case the Red Wing player gets past Bobby.

The Bruins still came in last during that season. But the fans didn't blame Bobby. He was the best anyone had seen. He received the Calder Memorial Trophy that year. This is an award given to the best new player of the season.

During Bobby's second season with the Bruins, some new players were added to the team. They were Phil Esposito, Fred Stanfield, and Ken Hodge. They had been players with the Chicago Black Hawks team. The Black Hawks had been a winning team. There was also a young player named Derek Sanderson. With Bobby and these new players, the Bruins team was now in good shape to start winning games.

Bobby is ready for action against the Montreal Canadiens.

Some fans expected Bobby to make the Bruins a winning team by himself. But hockey is a team game. It must have good players working together to win.

Phil Esposito is in the center.
He and the other Bruin players
praise Bobby for scoring.

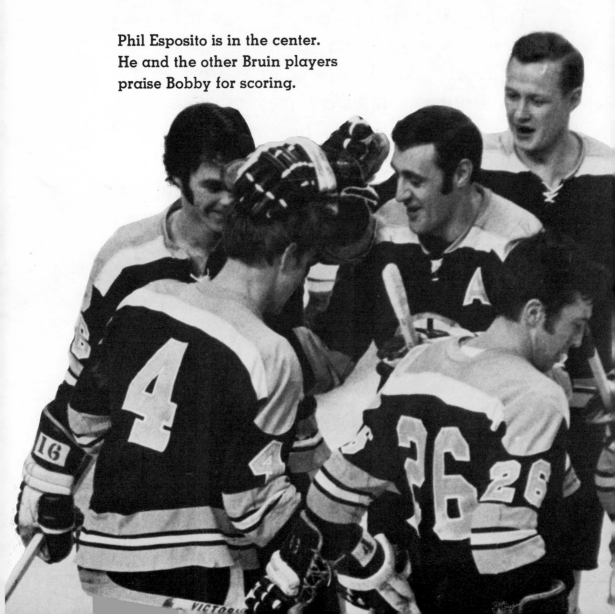

Sometimes they fight together.
Hockey is a game, but it can be rough.

The Boston Bruins finished in third place in the hockey league in 1967–68. It was Bobby's second season with them. They were sure that in a few more years they would win the Stanley Cup.

The Stanley Cup is a big trophy. It is given to the team that wins the Stanley Cup tournament at the end of the season. The tournament is just like the World Series in baseball. Seven games may be played. The team that first wins four games is the National Hockey League champion.

Bobby had hurt his knees during the 1967–68 season. He had to miss several Bruins games. But often Bobby would play when his knees hurt him badly. He wanted to help his team win.

Bobby lying on the ice because his knee is badly hurt. Since 1967 he has had many operations. Bobby could not play part of the 1976 season because of his knees.

The Bruins had their chance to play for the Stanley Cup during the 1969–70 season. They beat the New York Rangers team and the Chicago Black Hawks.

This made them the champions in their part of the National Hockey League. Now they would be playing the St. Louis Blues. This was for the Stanley Cup.

The Boston Bruins had not won the Stanley Cup since 1941. The fans and the team really wanted to win it in 1970.

Bobby Orr (in white) gives Bobby Hull of the Chicago Black Hawks a check to keep him from scoring.

On May 10, 1970, in Boston Garden, the Boston Bruins faced the St. Louis Blues for the fourth game of the series. The Bruins had won all three of the games played so far. If they won this fourth one, the Stanley Cup would be theirs.

The Bruins made the first goal and led the game 1 to 0. Then St. Louis made two goals and were leading. The Bruins scored again. Then St. Louis.

With only seven minutes to go in the game, the Bruins scored again. Now it was 3 to 3. The game had to go into overtime. If the Bruins made the first goal, they would be the new Stanley Cup champions.

Bobby hits his famous slap shot. Sometimes the puck goes flying at 100 miles per hour.

Bobby trips, but is up in the air with joy. He has just made the goal that won the Stanley Cup for the Boston Bruins.

The referee dropped the puck during the face-off. Derek Sanderson passed it to Bobby. Then Derek quickly skated to a corner of the rink that was not guarded. Bobby passed the puck back to Derek. Then Bobby flashed toward the St. Louis net.

Derek shot the puck to Bobby, who was still moving toward the St. Louis cage. Bobby skated around the players of the other team. They were trying to stop him. He caught the puck on his stick. Wham! He shot it toward the net. Just as Bobby made the shot, one of the men on the St. Louis team tripped him. He went flying up in the air. But before he landed, he saw his puck go into the St. Louis goal. Flash! The red light went on! Goal! Boston had won the Stanley Cup.

Bobby had also been the highest scorer for the Bruins during this 1969–70 season. It was the first time a player who played defense had ever been first in scoring.

The Bruins lost the Stanley Cup the next year to the Montreal Canadiens. But the team set more than a dozen scoring records that year. Now Bobby has set records, too.

He became the first player ever to score more than 100 points two seasons in a row.

He won the trophy for best defenseman eight years in a row.

He was named the league's most valuable player three years in a row.

The Stanley Cup overflows with champagne. The Bruins celebrated their win right after the game.

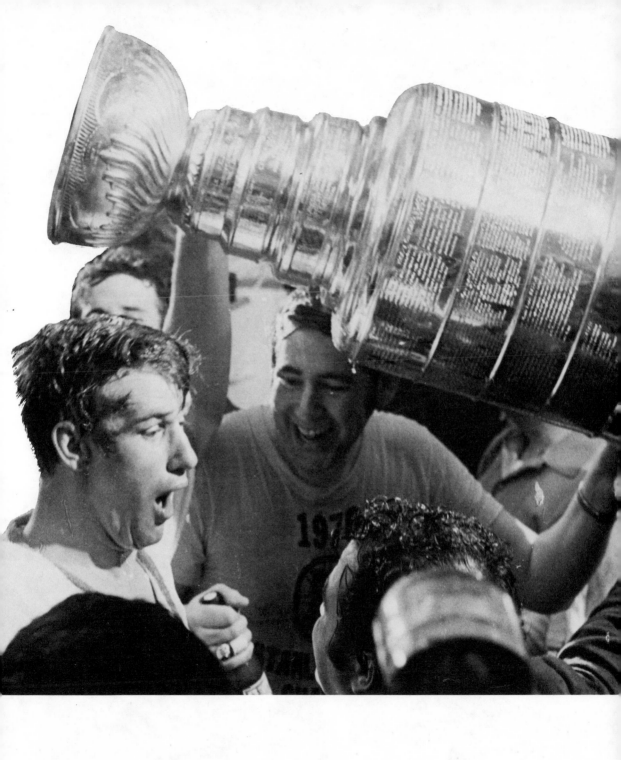

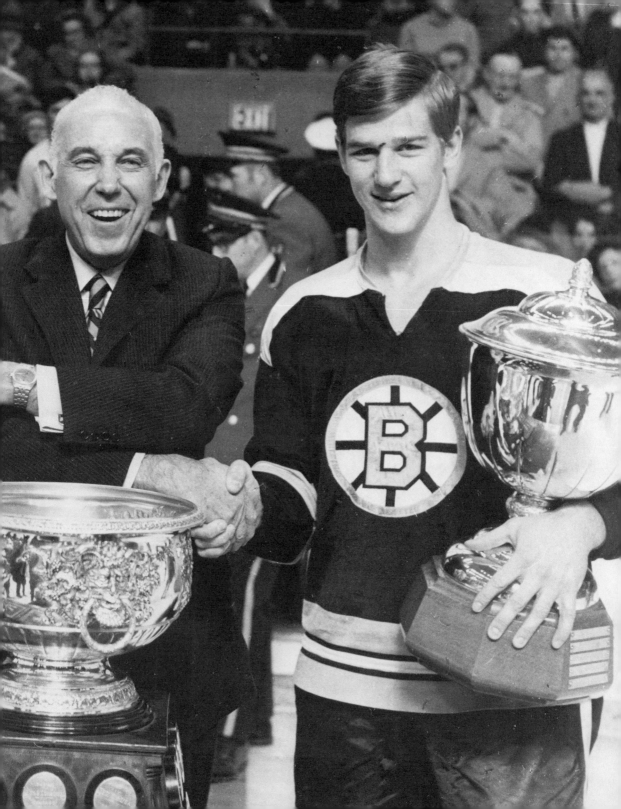

In 1972 Bobby helped the Bruins to win the Stanley Cup again. The team had won the cup two times in three years. They were now truly the "big, bad Bruins," as they liked to call themselves.

Bobby with National Hockey League
president Clarence M. Campbell,
receiving two of his many awards.
Here, they are the Norris Trophy,
for best defenseman, and the
Art Ross Trophy, for top scorer.

When he is off the skating rink, Bobby is shy and quiet. He likes to keep his home life to himself. He and his wife, Peggy, and their son spend their summers in Canada. Bobby and two friends run a camp there for boys. They teach the boys to play hockey.

Will any of these boys grow up to be another Bobby Orr? Like Bobby, they are learning to play the game early.

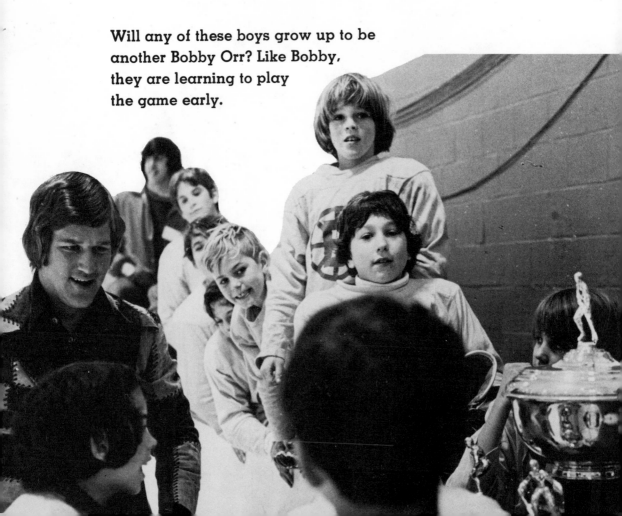

Bobby spends as much time as
possible with his son, Darren.

Bobby also gives much of his time to helping other people. He often visits hospitals and schools for sick or hurt children.

"I've been lucky," he says. "But a lot of people have not been so lucky. When I see some little girl who can't walk, but who keeps on smiling at me, I don't think I'm such a big hero anymore."

Bobby Orr left the big, bad Bruins team in 1976. He went to play with the Chicago Black Hawks. But he will be a good player wherever he is.

Bobby with one of his fans, Paula Pfeifer, the March of Dimes poster child for 1973.

ABOUT
THE AUTHORS

Audrey Edwards is a reporter who has worked as a magazine and news editor and a free-lance writer. She received a master's degree in education from Columbia University. But she says she got her real education through travels in Africa, the Caribbean, and Japan. Ms. Edwards says, "The next best thing to traveling is reading."

Gary Wohl was born in Newark, New Jersey. He attended New York University and has taught English, reading, and history to high school students. He has also taught reading in the Peace Corps and to the early elementary grades. Mr. Wohl's hobbies are all sports.

His most recent book, a collection of short Latin biographies, called *Latin Roots,* will be out in the fall.